TABLE OF CONTENTS

SUMMARY

Since 1956 France has made a concerted effort to develop its own nuclear weapons and the strategic capability to deliver them. This effort has now succeeded in bringing into existence the first elements of an all French nuclear delivery force called the _force de frappe_. It is the purpose of this paper to appraise the capabilities of this force and its implications for the United States.

Examination of the early history of the French nuclear weapon development program reveals that its original military requirement was changed to a political one with the return to power in 1958 of General de Gaulle. This increased emphasis resulted in the detonation of the first French nuclear device in February 1960. By 1962 this first device had been converted into a 60 kiloton, plutonium weapon suitable for delivery by the Mirage-IV aircraft being developed specifically for that purpose. Current French weapon development effort is directed toward development of a thermonuclear weapon. While there is ample evidence that the French unofficially sought US assistance in their weapon development, such assistance was not offered due to the general intransigence of General de Gaulle toward the United States.

The force being developed by the French to deliver its nuclear weapons is to consist of three generations. The first generation which is now entering operation consists of about 50 Mirage-IVA aircraft. The second will consist of 50 to 100 surface-to-surface ballistic missiles and will become operational starting in 1968. The third generation will consist of three nuclear submarines armed with Polaris type ballistic missiles to be operational by 1973.

Analysis of the effectiveness of the force indicates that the first generation is incapable of implementing the French strategy of proportional deterrence against the Soviet Union due to its small numbers, insufficient range, and inability to penetrate defenses. The second and third generations will be more effective but will lack sufficient numbers to deter the Soviet Union without outside assistance. The most significant effect of the _force de frappe_ on US strategy is the possibility that the French could use its launch to trigger the launch of a US strike against the Soviet Union.

This paper concludes by proposing that the United States adopt a policy of supporting and assisting the development of the _force de frappe_ into a militarily effective instrument provided the French place the force under NATO control except where vital French national interests are at stake.

CHAPTER 1

INTRODUCTION

THE PROBLEM

The nuclear strength of the free world has been provided for over 20 years by the United States. Some small assistance was provided in the last eight years of this period by the United Kingdom. In 1965 the United States maintained 5000 nuclear weapons in Europe in support of the North Atlantic Alliance forces and maintained more than 5000 additional nuclear weapons for use by its own strategic forces.[1] In spite of this strength, France has found it necessary to develop its own nuclear weapons and delivery vehicles to be used independently in what they call their force de frappe. Why has such costly duplication taken place between two of the world's oldest allies? What does this force de frappe consist of? What military purposes does this force serve? What effects will the French force have on US and NATO strategies? This paper is an attempt to answer the above essentially military questions without becoming unduly involved in the maze of political problems now facing the United States, France, and the rest of NATO.

---

[1]Henry Tanner, "5,000 A-Warheads Stored for NATO, McNamara Says," New York Times, 28 Nov. 1965, p. 1.

However, since the political and military problems cannot be completely separated, those political problems most directly related to the force de frappe must be considered.

PURPOSE AND SCOPE

This paper appraises the implications for the United States of France's attainment of an independent nuclear weapon delivery capability. First, the French nuclear weapon program is reviewed with emphasis on France's reasons for undertaking the program. The development of delivery systems for the nuclear weapons is then reviewed in order to identify its characteristics effecting the military capability of the force which the systems make up. An analysis of the capability of the French force to implement their stated strategy is then made. From this analysis an estimate of the effects of the French force on US and NATO strategy is made. Finally, conclusions are drawn as to military value of the force in its present and future forms and a recommendation is made for US action to take advantage of the French capability.

The reader is cautioned that this paper is based entirely on unclassified information and therefore is limited to "facts" as found in the open literature. Since the Atomic Energy Act does not differentiate between information concerning US nuclear weapons and those of other nations; the unclassified sources of all information concerning the design, development, fabrication, and utilization of nuclear weapons used in this paper are carefully cited.

CHAPTER 2

THE FRENCH NUCLEAR WEAPONS PROGRAM

HISTORY

The foundation for the French nuclear weapons program was established by a decree issued on 8 October 1945 by the Provisional Government of France. This decree established the French Atomic Energy Commission or Commissareat 'a l' Energie Atomique (CEA) and gave it the mission of developing the uses of atomic energy in the fields of science, industry, and defense.[1] While the mission given to the CEA is quite similar to that given the US Atomic Energy Commission (AEC), the CEA came into existence over two months prior to the introduction in the US Congress of what later became the Atomic Energy Act of 1946 establishing the AEC.[2]

During the first five years of its existence the CEA devoted most of its efforts to procurement and refinement of fissionable materials, development of research reactors, and the training of research personnel. Little or no effort was devoted to the military aspects of atomic energy. The first High Commissioner of the CEA was Frederic Joliot, the husband of Irene Curie. Since Joliot had been a member of the Communist Party and was known to hold

---

[1]Embassy of France, Press Service, France's First Atomic Explosion, p. 5.
[2]U.S. Congress, JCAE, Atomic Energy Legislation Through 88th Congress, 2nd Session, p. 237. (Hereafter referred to as "Atomic Energy Legislation".)

Communist views, some French writers attribute the CEA's lack of attention to military aspects to Joliot's presence as High Commissioner from 1945 to 1950.[3]

According to the French White Paper on France's first atomic explosion, those concerned with national defense in France became aware of the military nuclear facts in 1951.[4] Studies conducted by the French military about this time concluded that nuclear armaments were perfectly conceivable for a country such as France. In October 1954 the military established a Comite des Explosifs Nucleaires and attached its members to the CEA.[5] Thus, the organizational basis of a nuclear weapon development program was established. From 1954 through 1956 all of France was debating whether France should develop nuclear weapons. In spite of this debate another important step toward the development of French nuclear weapons was taken on 10 May 1955. On that date the Ministers of Armed Forces, Finance, and Atomic Power signed a document ordering the armed forces to transfer to the CEA funds for the expansion of the Reactor Center at Marcoule for the production and separation of plutonium. Marcoule was established under the CEA's first five year plan (1952-1957) and included two reactors for the experimental production of electric power. This decree established a third reactor and gave all Marcoule reactors

---

[3]Marc de Lacaste Lareymondie, French Nuclear Power, p. 3.
[4]Embassy of France, Press Service, op. cit., p. 7.
[5]Ciro E. Zoppo, France as a Nuclear Power, p. 4.

the primary mission of the production of plutonium. The new program included a plant for the chemical separation of plutonium. Thus, on 10 May 1955 it was determined that France would produce plutonium on a large scale while the only possible use for such a product was nuclear weapons. This decree also determined, without specifically stating it, that any French weapons program would be run by the CEA and not the military.[6]

The debate within France concerning development of nuclear weapons continued through most of 1956. During this time the weapons program went underground within the CEA in the form of a cover organization called Bureau of General Studies. This organization proceeded with recruitment of personnel, purchasing of the necessary land, construction of laboratories, and completion of the research studies--all of which were essential to a weapons development program. This organization did not come fully out into the open until 1958 when it became the Direction des Applications Militaires (DAM) which is the French equivalent of the US Atomic Energy Commission's Division of Military Application (DMA).[7] Finally, after much debate in which many details of the underground program leaked out, the Mollet government decided to proceed with the development of a French nuclear weapon. The decision took the form of a new protocol dated 30 November 1956 which replaced that of 20 May 1955. This document was signed by the

---

[6]Lareymondie, op. cit., pp. 4-6.
[7]Lareymondie, op. cit., pp. 6-7.

Minister of National Defense and the Secretary of State, Atomic Energy, and established a nuclear weapon development and testing program for the period 1957 through 1961. The protocol assigned the CEA the following responsibilities:

a. Conducting the preliminary studies for the experimental atomic explosions.

b. Preparing the scientific parts of the tests.

c. Supplying the necessary plutonium.

d. Making prototypes.

e. Carrying out experimental atomic explosions.

The armed services were made responsible for the preparation for experiments concerning nuclear explosions and placed in charge of the testing area. This same document assigned the CEA the task of making studies leading to the construction of a factory for the separation of uranium 235 and to the supply of highly enriched uranium.[8] Thus, the French program included not only the development and testing of a plutonium weapon but also provided for procurement of U-235 for an advanced weapon program.

With the overall policy having been defined by the government, the CEA and the Armed Services proceeded to organize the joint structure necessary to fabricate and test nuclear weapons. These organizations received their general instructions by means of a resolution signed by the Premier on 11 April 1958 ordering that

---

[8]Embassy of France, Press Service, op. cit., p. 9.

measures be taken to execute, upon order from the Government, the first series of "military atomic device test explosions" beginning in the first quarter of 1960. Due to the fall of the Fourth Republic and the return of General de Gaulle to power in May 1958, another resolution was signed by Premier de Gaulle on 22 July 1958 setting the date for the first experimental explosion as the first quarter of 1960.[9] These two resolutions make a point often missed in current literature. That is, the French nuclear weapons program is not a product of General de Gaulle and the Fifth Republic. He inherited the program from the Fourth Republic but immediately endorsed it.

RESULTS

The efforts of the CEA and the Armed Forces resulted in France's first test of a nuclear device on 13 February 1960 at Reggan in the Sahara Desert portion of Algeria. With this explosion France became the world's fourth nuclear power. The French announcement of the test frankly referred to the device as "this plutonium bomb."[10] This is not surprising since the construction of the plant for the separation of U-235 called for by the original program had only recently begun at Pierrelatte. Thus, plutonium from the reactors at Marcoule was the only fissionable material available for this test. The United States reports the yield of

---

[9]Ibid., p. 11.
[10]Embassy of France, Press Service, op. cit., p. 1.

the first French device as 60-70 kilotons.[11] This first test was followed by three more atmospheric tests of smaller yields at Reggan with the last taking place on 25 April 1961.[12] Since that date, all French tests have been conducted underground at Hoggar, also in Algeria. The most notable of these was that conducted on 1 May 1962 which the French announced as a test of a prototype of the weapon to be carried by the Mirage-IV aircraft. The yield of the test was specified as 50 kilotons.[13] When this weapon became operational, the French government permitted Paris-Match to publish a photograph of it in its now famous 15 May 1965 edition.[14] Since Paris-Match referred to the photographed weapon as "the French bomb," it seems reasonable to conclude that as of 15 May 1965, only one French nuclear weapon existed. The following summarizes the published characteristics of this weapon:

     Weight - a little more than 2,000 pounds
     Length - about four meters
     Yield - 60 kilotons
     Delivery method - Free-fall from Mirage-IV aircraft
     Number available - Equal to number of Mirage-IV's.[15]

Due to the debate in France concerning the French nuclear weapons program, the unclassified literature is full of information concerning French efforts to develop advanced nuclear weapons including thermonuclear weapons. The most important indicators of

---

[11]Effects of Nuclear Weapons, p. 679.
[12]Ibid.
[13]Lareymondie, op. cit., p. 15.
[14]"Here is the French Atomic Force," Paris-Match, 15 May 1965, p. VIII.
[15]Ibid.

8

this program are the continued appropriation of large sums for the completion of the U-235 separation plant at Pierrelatte and for completion of the Pacific Nuclear Test Center at Mururoa Atoll. These items were included in the Second Military Program Law approved by the French Parliament in December 1964.[16] The Pacific Nuclear Test Center has been under construction since 1962 and is expected to be ready for its first test in 1966. Design of some of the installations at the Center indicates that nuclear devices with yields up to one megaton will be tested there.[17]

The Pierrelatte plant for separation of U-235 will consist of four separate stages. Only the first stage which provides a product enriched to 2% in U-235 is now in operation. The other three stages will progressively enrich the product to 90% U-235. The full plant is expected to be in operation in 1967.[18]

In addition to the 60 kiloton nuclear weapon now operational with Mirage IV aircraft, the French press also provides some characteristics of the advanced weapons being developed by the French. The latest information indicates the development of two additional warheads for use with French ballistic missiles. The first of these is a "beefed-up" version of the existing bomb to provide an all plutonium warhead of about 350 kiloton yield for

---

[16]"Messmer Explains Objectives of Program," Press Reports and Commentary on French Nuclear Developments, JPRS 28192, p. 53.

[17]New French Nuclear Test Center in Polynesia, JPRS 964, pp. 1-3.

[18]J. Pergent, Two Thousand French Atomic Bombs in 1970, JPRS 28192, p. 40.

delivery by the ground based, solid fuel ballistic missile. The other warhead discussed by the French press is a thermonuclear warhead using U-235 for delivery by the submarine launched ballistic missile now under development. This latter warhead would also replace the 350 kiloton warhead when sufficient U-235 is available.[19] While no unclassified estimate of the yield of the thermonuclear warhead is available, the design specifications discussed above for the Pacific Test Center indicate a yield of about one megaton is expected.

Thus, the unclassified French literature indicates that the present French weapons program consists of the following weapons:

    a. An existing 60 kiloton free-fall bomb for the Mirage IV.

    b. A 350 kiloton warhead under development for the ground based ballistic missile.

    c. A thermonuclear warhead of about one megaton under development for the submarine launched ballistic missile.

WHY

No discussion of the French development of nuclear weapons would be complete without inclusion of the French reasons for pursuing such an expensive program at a time when the nuclear

---

[19]Nicholas Vichney, French Science, Technology, and Industry Vis-A-Vis the Nuclear Deterrent Force," JPRS 28192, p. 4.

strength of the United States was universally recognized as the sole provider of the security of all the West including France. The initial (1956) decision of the Mollet government to develop and test a weapon must be attributed to the efforts of the French military who simply maintained that no defense was possible without nuclear weapons. The leader of these military crusaders was General Pierre Gallois of the Air Force. General Gallois, although now retired from the Air Force, continues his prolific writing in support of an independent French nuclear force. However, his credibility is now much less due to the fact that his present employer is Dassalt Aircraft, the manufacturer of Mirage-IV aircraft. Gallois' original thesis was that the nuclear weapon would serve as the equalizer between the large powers and the small powers. He maintained as early as 1954 that French capability to destroy as few as 20 Soviet cities would deter Soviet aggression against France.[20] This same reasoning was adopted by General de Gaulle and his associates upon return to power in June 1958. General de Gaulle added to the defense theory the proposition that an independent nuclear deterrent had become a necessary attribute of a major power. A later addition of President de Gaulle and his Defense Minister, Pierre Messmer, was that France can no longer count on the US nuclear force being used to protect

---

[20]Robert Kleiman, "What France Is Out to Get," Reader's Digest, January 1964, p. 102.

11

France (and NATO) because of the vulnerability of the United States itself to Soviet ICBM's.

US ASSISTANCE

A factor which may have expedited the French weapons program in the 1958 to 1960 period was the possibility of United States assistance in the design and fabrication of French weapons. In January 1958, at the request of the Eisenhower Administration, there was introduced into the Congress a proposal to amend the Atomic Energy Act of 1954 to allow exchange of US information concerning the design and fabrication of nuclear weapons with certain qualified friendly nations. This proposal also included a provision to allow furnishing of unfabricated plutonium and enriched uranium to friendly nations for use in weapons. In the hearings and debates concerning this legislation, it was quite clear that the United Kingdom was the only nation with which such cooperation was intended. Therefore, a stipulation was written into the law that nuclear weapon design information could only be exchanged with nations that had made "substantial progress in the development of atomic weapons." At that time the United Kingdom was the only ally of the United States that could so qualify.[21] This proposal became Sections 144c and 91c of the Atomic Energy Act of

---

[21]Hearings before the Subcommittee on Agreements for Cooperation of the Joint Committee on Atomic Energy, 85th Congress, 2nd Session, pp. 2 and 263. (Referred to hereafter as JCAE Hearings.)

1954, as amended, on July 2, 1958.[22] On the following day the United States and the United Kingdom signed an agreement providing for exchange of weapon information to the limits of the amended law.[23] Thus, the French were put on notice that although the United States was helping the UK weapons program, there could be no assistance to France until France had made substantial progress in the development of nuclear weapons. While the determination that a nation has made substantial progress is left to the President, the Joint Committee on Atomic Energy in reporting the bill to Congress made its intentions clear with these words:

> It is intended that the cooperating nation must have achieved a capability on its own of fabricating a variety of atomic weapons, and constructed and operated the necessary facilities, including weapons research and development laboratories weapon-manufacturing facilities, a weapon testing station, and trained personnel to operate each of these facilities.[24]

It also must have been obvious to the French that a number of nuclear tests were required since the United Kingdom had detonated 17 nuclear devices (including two in the megaton range) by the time the agreement was signed.[25] It seems certain that the French were disappointed that US assistance to them was precluded while it was readily given to the United Kingdom. This situation in 1958 was the start of the nuclear phase of the favored nation

---

[22]Atomic Energy Legislation, op. cit., p. 207.

[23]U.S. Dept. of State, United States Treaties and Other International Agreements, Vol. 9, 1958, p. 1028.

[24]Amendment to the Atomic Energy Act of 1954, as Amended, House Report No. 1849, 5 June 1958, p. 12.

[25]Effects of Nuclear Weapons, op. cit.

relationship between the United States and the United Kingdom which has always been distasteful to the French. In fact, a strong case can be made that the special nuclear relationship between the United States and United Kingdom is the basic cause of most of the present difficulties between France and the United States and France and the United Kingdom.[26] General de Gaulle's sensitivity on the subject of US assistance to the British weapons program is best illustrated by the following comment that he made upon being shown a prototype of the first French weapon in December 1959: "Now, the really important thing here, you see, is the fact that we have done this by ourselves--and I mean: All by ourselves."[27]

After the French nuclear tests in 1960 and 1961, many expected that US assistance to the French weapons program would be forthcoming. There was now a new US President who had a good basis for determining that France had now made substantial progress on the development of nuclear weapons and thereby qualified for US assistance under Section 144c of the Atomic Energy Act. Such arrangements have never been consumated. The most obvious reason for this is that the French never made a formal request to the United States for such aid. General de Gaulle was careful to point out this fact in his famous press conference of 14 January

----

[26]Wolfgang J. Lehmann, The Anglo-American "Special" Nuclear Relationship Implications and Consequences, pp. 1-59.
[27]Charles de Gaulle, as quoted by Marc Lareymondie, op. cit., p. 11.

14

1963 where, in condemning the US-UK Nassau Arrangements, he said:

> To build these submarines and warheads, the British
> receive privileged assistance from the Americans. You
> know--I say this in passing--that this assistance was
> never offered to us and you should know, despite what
> some report, that we have never asked for it.[28]

While General de Gaulle is correct in saying he had never requested

such aid, there were a number of informal requests made in his

behalf. The New York Times reported on 10 April 1960 (only eight

weeks after the first French test) that the French Ambassador in

Washington was feeling out the members of the Joint Committee on

Atomic Energy concerning a Section 144c Agreement for France.[29]

Since nothing further transpired, it seems a fair assumption that

the Committee did not encourage the Ambassador. In addition,

President Kennedy's biographer, Theodore Sorensen, reports that

President Kennedy rejected nuclear weapons aid to France on two

occasions. According to Mr. Sorensen, such aid to France was

recommended to the President by the Secretary of Defense and the

US Ambassador to France in 1962 but was opposed by the State

Department and most of the White House staff. President Kennedy

rejected the proposal because such aid would not win de Gaulle to

our purposes but only strengthen him in his.[30] Mr. Sorensen also

reports that after the Nassau Conference of December 1962, Presi-

dent Kennedy was prepared to provide (among other things) nuclear

weapons aid to France if the French would align their nuclear

[28]Charles de Gaulle, Speeches and Press Conferences, No. 185,
p. 11.
[29]John Finney, "France is Seeking 'Atomic Club' Seat," New
York Times, 10 April 1960, p. 1.
[30]Theodore Sorensen, Kennedy, p. 572.

delivery forces under NATO. While this was a complete reversal on the President's part, General de Gaulle's hostile rejection of the Nassau Arrangements made serious negotiations impossible.[31] Although the offer was never made, its proposal indicates that President Kennedy was willing to make the determination that France had made substantial progress in the development of nuclear weapons and therefore met the statutory requirement for US nuclear assistance.

While US nuclear weapons aid to France has not materialized, the advantages to France from access to US weapons technology and enriched uranium would be enormous. If such aid were available, the French thermonuclear weapon development program, their Pacific Test Center, and their Pierrelatte enriched uranium plant would probably not be necessary.

---

[31]Ibid., p. 273.

CHAPTER 3

FRENCH DELIVERY VEHICLES

THE PROGRAMS

The French program to develop nuclear weapons caused little
or no controversy through 1959. The French had been quietly
working on a manned aircraft for delivery of their nuclear weapons.
However, General de Gaulle put greater emphasis than his predeces-
sors on the military and political roles of a French nuclear
weapon. In a speech to the Center of Higher Military Studies and
the three combined military service academies on 3 November 1959,
General de Gaulle outlined a new defense policy for France with
these words:

> The defense of France must be in French hands. A
> country, such as France, must be able to fight its
> own wars, if it should ever have to fight a war. Of
> course, French defense, depending on the particular
> case, will be combined with the defense of other
> countries. This is the nature of things. But it is
> absolutely necessary that we have our own defense,
> that France can defend herself, by herself, for her-
> self, and in her own fashion.
>
> If this were any different--if the situation were to
> continue the way it has been, if the defense of France
> were taken out of the national framework and confused
> with something else--then we would no longer have a
> country or a state. The government exists for the
> purpose of directing the defense of the independence
> and integrity of the territory of France, at any time.
> This so-called system of "integration" which has been
> inaugurated and which to some extent, was even imple-
> mented after the great trials we have gone through,
> this system, which was established at a time when
> there was a reason to believe that the free world was
> facing an imminent and unlimited threat, at a time
> when we had not yet recovered our national personality,

17

this system has now seen its day. As a consequence, we must obviously, during the coming years, build a force capable of taking action for ourselves, a force which we have come to call the "striking force" (force de frappe), a force which will be capable of going into action at any moment, anywhere. It goes without saying that this force will be based on atomic weapons --atomic weapons which we will either make ourselves or purchase someplace, but which will belong to us, one way or another; and since someone is capable of destroying France, possibly, from some place on earth, we must equip our force so that it will be able to hit any point on earth.[1]

With these words, General de Gaulle, not only prescribed the defense policy of France but also wrote the charter for the force de frappe, a French strategic force armed with nuclear weapons capable of striking any place on earth. General de Gaulle did not say how many places on earth had to be hit or what effectiveness was required. This was to come several years later, probably after the price of such a force had been investigated. Some experts feel that General de Gaulle's reference to the possibility of France's purchasing nuclear weapons was a direct hint to American policy makers to grant France nuclear weapons aid with a Section 144c agreement.[2] The hint did not take; however, it is obvious from this speech that General de Gaulle wanted the weapons completely under French control. A weapons aid agreement under Section 144c of the Atomic Energy Act would allow that control since, as Senator Clinton Anderson so ably put it, such cooperation

---

[1]Charles de Gaulle, as quoted by Marc Lareymondie, French Nuclear Power, pp. 10-11.

[2]Ciro E. Zoppo, France as a Nuclear Power, p. 10.

18

simply provides the recipient with a do-it-yourself kit for US
nuclear weapons.[3]

First implementation of General de Gaulle's requirement for
the _force de frappe_ was authorized by the French Parliament on
6 December 1960 with the passing of the First French Armament
Program or "Program Law" as the French call it. This program was
subjected to seven weeks of raging debate in the French Parliament and was twice defeated in the Senate. However, it was
adopted automatically after the third and final reading by the
Assembly.[4] This program was a transitional one covering the
period 1960-1964. It envisioned three generations of the _force
de frappe_. The first, which was actually authorized, was to
consist of the Mirage-IVA aircraft armed with the free-fall nuclear
bomb being developed for it by the CEA. The second generation,
for which the program authorized initial studies, was to consist
of ground-to-ground ballistic missiles armed with the second
generation nuclear warhead being developed by the CEA. The third
generation was to be submarine launched ballistic missiles armed
with the thermonuclear warhead included in the CEA's development
program.[5]

The "Second Program Law" covering 1965-1970 was approved by
the Parliament in December 1964 and made firm the second and third

---

[3]JCAE Hearings, p. 102.
[4]Zoppo, op. cit., p. 12.
[5]"France's Force de Frappe," Interavia, June 1964, p. 799.
(Hereafter referred to as "Interavia.")

19

generations. In explaining the program, Pierre Messmer, Minister of the Armed Forces, included the following as an objective of the program:

> Development of the strategic nuclear weapons by completing operations written into the 1960 law, and by launching operations required for the acquisition of thermonuclear weapons.[6]

Based on this second program, the current French press describes the three generations of the force de frappe as follows:

a. The first generation is composed of 62 Mirage-IVA aircraft each carrying a 60 kiloton fission bomb. Operational life will be 1965 to 1971.

b. The second generation will consist of 50 to 100 surface-to-surface ballistic missiles equipped with an enriched uranium warhead of 300 kilotons. Operational life expected to be 1968 to 1978.

c. The third generation will consist of three nuclear propelled submarines armed with Polaris type ballistic missiles with thermonuclear warheads. Operational life is expected to be 1969-1985.[7]

THE MIRAGE-IVA AIRCRAFT

In November of 1964 the first generation of the force de frappe became operational with the delivery of Mirage-IVA aircraft

---

[6]Pierre Messmer, as quoted in Messmer Explains Objectives of Program, JPRS 28192, p. 52.

[7]French Deterrent Force Armament Plan, JPRS GUO:942, p. 26.

to the French Strategic Air Command (Commandement Aeirennes Strategiques, called CAS by the French). A total of 62 of these aircraft are to be delivered by the middle of 1966 providing an operational capability of about 50 aircraft.[8] Since these aircraft each armed with one of the 60 kiloton bombs previously described will constitute the entire French strategic capability at least until 1968, their effectiveness determines the immediate credibility of the force de frappe. Therefore, the characteristics of this aircraft must be examined.

The Mirage-IVA was conceived in 1957 which, as in the case of the French nuclear weapon program, was prior to General de Gaulle's return to power. It was developed and is being produced by Dassault Aircraft (Generale Aeronautique Marcel Dassault) who evolved it directly out of their successful development of the Mirage-III, a Mach 2 interceptor operational with the French Air Force. The Mirage-IVA is a direct scale-up of the interceptor, being about one and a half times its size. This scale-up approach was adopted by the French as the fastest way of producing a strategic bomber.[9]

The Mirage-IVA is a delta winged, two place aircraft weighing about 66,000 pounds. It is powered by two SNECMA Atar 9K afterburning engines, each producing 15,000 pounds of thrust. Its

---

[8]"French Continue Nuclear Delivery Buildup in 6 Year Plan," Aviation Week and Space Technology, 15 Mar. 1965, p. 271.
[9]Richard Clayton Peet, "De Gaulle's Force De Dissuasion," Air Force and Space Digest, June 1964, pp. 30-31.

21

maximum speed is Mach 2.2. The mission profile includes a high-altitude cruise for much of its mission at Mach 1.7. This performance was demonstrated in the test flight program. Its ceiling is in excess of 60,000 feet. The crew consists of a pilot and a navigator seated in tandem. The Mirage-IVA carries one of the French 60 kiloton nuclear bombs under its center section, partly recessed into the fuselage. Its primary mode of delivery of that weapon is to descend to low altitude, make a high speed run to the target, and release the weapon in a preprogrammed toss maneuver. High and medium altitude bombing capabilities are also provided. The bombing-navigation system includes capabilities for inertial navigation, radar bombing, and terrain avoidance.[10]

The range of the Mirage-IVA has been a problem from the start. Any discussions of the range of the Mirage IVA as released by the French must be prefaced by the fact that the distance from the nearest point on the French-West German border to Moscow is 1040 nautical miles (1200 statute miles). Another pertinent fact is that the distance from the only publicly announced base of the Mirage-IVA, Mont de Masan (south of Bordeaux),[11] is 1500 nautical miles (1710 statute miles).

With internal fuel only, the range of the Mirage-IVA is only 1000 statute miles on its high altitude profile. Since this would

_____

10Mirage IV parameters cited are from Peet, op. cit.; and Interavia, op. cit.
11"Here Is The French Atomic Force," Paris-Match, 15 May 1965, p. I. (Hereafter referred to as Paris-Match.)

allow only one way missions to Soviet targets, two 550 gallon wing tanks were added.[12] With these tanks the French claim a range of 1550 statute miles (1350 nautical miles).[13] Since this was only about one-half the range required for a two-way mission on Moscow, the French were forced to add an inflight refueling capability. Twelve KC-135 tanker aircraft were therefore purchased from the United States and became operational with the CAS in 1964. With one refueling the French claim a range of "nearly 3,000 miles" for the Mirage-IVA.[14] This range of 3,000 miles (2,600 nautical miles) is confirmed by recent unclassified US literature for high altitude missions with refueling.[15] While the Mirage IVA has been provided the equipment necessary for low altitude missions which are believed necessary to penetrate modern air defenses, no information has been released concerning the range of the aircraft on such a mission. However, based on the low altitude performance of similar turbojet aircraft, a generous estimate would be that the range would be degraded by a factor of two if the mission is below 5,000 feet.[16] Then, this writer's estimate of the inflight refueled (one refueling) range of the Mirage-IVA is 3,000 statute miles (2,600 nautical miles)

---

[12]Peet, op. cit., p. 31.

[13]"France and Its Armed Forces," Embassy of France, Dec. 1964, p. 9.

[14]Ibid.

[15]"Aviation Week," op. cit.

[16]An unclassified example of low altitude range degradation is that the T-33 will go 2 nautical miles on one gallon of fuel at 40,000 feet and only .9 nautical mile on one gallon at 10,000 feet.

for its high altitude mission and 1,600 nautical miles (1,820 statute miles) for its high-low-high altitude mission where one-third of the mission is below 5,000 feet.

The designers of the Mirage-IVA were careful to adhere to the design specification that the aircraft be capable of operating from existing airfields. It can operate from a 6,000 foot dirt runway hardened by chemical spray. There are some 78 airfields in France which exceed this specification.[17]

To provide command and control for the Mirage-IVA force, the French have constructed an underground command post at Taverny about 20 miles from Paris. Here, some forty meters underground, the strike order would be given to all bases of the _force de frappe_. Both the commander of CAS and his deputy must receive parts of a launch order from the President of the Republic before launch can be ordered. In addition, each of the two crew members on the aircraft must receive a proper code number and place it on a special keyboard before the nuclear weapon on the aircraft can be armed.[18] There are two distinct chains of command, one for launching the aircraft, the other for releasing the weapons.[19]

The French government was very careful to inform the world when the first elements of the _force de frappe_ became operational. First, a much publicized picture story of the first Mirage-IVA's

[17]Interavia, _op. cit._, p. 801.
[18]Paris-Match, _op. cit._
[19]"France and Its Armed Forces," _op. cit._, p. 9.

was published in Paris-Match on 15 May 1965. This story included what was purported to be the world's first unclassified photograph of an operational nuclear weapon--the bomb for delivery by the Mirage-IVA.[20] Later on Bastille Day, 14 July 1965, 12 Mirage-IV's from the first two squadrens of the CAS were flown in formation over the Arc de Triomphe. These aircraft were followed by six of the KC-135 tankers.[21] In this manner the world was notified that the first generation of the force de frappe is operational.

THE SECOND GENERATION

Since its proposed submarine launched ballistic missile force cannot be fully operational before 1973, France found it necessary to introduce a surface launched ballistic missile force to fill the period (about 1969-1973) when the Mirage-IVA force will be questionable due to advances in air defense. Preliminary studies concerning such a missile were authorized in the first "Program Law" passed in 1960. As indicated above, the second "Program Law" included authority to develop and manufacture this missile. This missile, called SSBS for sol-sol balistique strategique (surface-to-surface strategic ballistic), will be a multi-stage, solid fueled missile, essentially a land based version of the submarine launched missile being developed for the third generation. The first SSBS is expected to become operational in 1968 with a 300

---

[20]Paris-Match, op. cit., p. 1.
[21]Peter Braestrup, New York Times, 15 Jul. 1965, p. 5.

25

kiloton warhead.[22] The number of missiles to be procured is
indefinite with estimates ranging from 50 to 100[23] down to 25.[24]
The French state the range of the SSBS will be about 2,000 statute
miles (1,720 nautical miles).[25] The missiles will be placed in
underground silos about 120 feet in depth. The location for these
silos was chosen in October 1965 as the Albion Plateau in south-
east France about 40 miles east of Avignon. Actual construction
of the silos will begin in April 1966 with the first five sites
to be operational during the first quarter of 1968. The missiles
are to be placed in batteries of ten with each battery having a
command post or launch control center. Construction plans indicate a total of 30 missile sites or three batteries. The silos
are very similar to the Minuteman missile silos now existing in
the United States.[26]

THE THIRD GENERATION

The third generation of the *force de frappe* will consist of
three nuclear powered submarines each carrying 16 underwater
launched ballistic missiles patterned after the US Polaris missile.
The French refer to this missile as the MSBS for *mersol balistique-
strategique* (underwater-to-surface strategic ballistic).

----

[22]French Deterrent Force Armament Plan, op. cit.
[23]Ibid.
[24]Aviation Week, op. cit.
[25]France and Its Armed Forces, op. cit., p. 52.
[26]Christian Reboul, First Strategic Rocket Bases Will Be Ready
in 1968, JPRS, GUO:935, 2 Nov. 1965, pp. 18-20.

The MSBS will be equipped with the thermonuclear warhead now under development by the French and is expected to have a range of about 1,500 statute miles (1,320 nautical miles).[27]

The French development programs for the submarine and its missile are extensive and amount to what may be called a duplication of the US Polaris program. A conventional submarine, the Gymnote, has been modified as an experimental launching platform to perfect underwater launching of the missile. A land based prototype of the nuclear reactor for the submarine has been constructed at the Cadarache Nuclear Research Center using enriched uranium furnished by the United States. This reactor went critical in August 1964 and the French are now testing the entire nuclear propulsion system for the submarine.[28] The French expect the first of the three MSBS submarines to be operational in 1969, with the remaining two becoming operational by 1973.[29] However, it should be pointed out that this program is dependent on the Pierrelatte uranium separation plant for enriched uranium both for its reactors and its weapons.

---

[27]French Deterrent Force Armament Plan, op. cit.
[28]France and Its Armed Forces, op. cit., p. 37.
[29]French Deterrent Force Armament Plan, op. cit.

CHAPTER 4

ASSESSMENT OF THE MILITARY CAPABILITY OF THE FORCE

THE STRATEGY

While this paper is devoted to the military aspects of the

independent nuclear capability of France, any discussion of the

strategy proposed for the employment of that capability must be

prefaced by some mention of the political motives behind its

creation. As mentioned above, much has been written concerning

the necessity of France's possession of an independent nuclear

capability in order to resume its position as a major world power

and to be treated as such in the North Atlantic Alliance. Such

a political motive could be the cause of the little attention

given to the effectiveness of the French force by French political

authorities. Professor Henry Kissinger supports their view with

these words:

> From the perspective of vindicating France's identity,
> de Gaulle is not so concerned with the technical aspects
> of strategy as with the political problems of choice.
> The United States considers central control over nuclear
> weapons crucial for the contingency of general war; de
> Gaulle gives priority to France's impact on the conduct
> of day-to-day diplomacy. Secretary McNamara strives for
> strategic options; President de Gaulle seeks political
> ones.[1]

Others say that it is quite clear that the purpose of the force de

frappe is its use as an instrument for French domination in Western

---

[1]Henry A. Kissinger, The Troubled Partnership, p. 54.

Europe and to keep Germany and Great Britain in a subordinate position.[2] Nevertheless, the expenditure of such large sums of money for a military force, even in a France led by General de Gaulle, requires justification in the form of a strategy by which the force would be employed. This, General de Gaulle and his associates have provided in the form of a strategy which provides a most welcome feature to French fiscal authorities. This bit of magic holds that the number of systems required for the force is approximately equal to whatever the French can afford. This strategy is a new degree of deterrence called proportional deterrence. General de Gaulle, after explaining that US nuclear power could no longer be counted on to protect France, justified the force de frappe and announced the strategy of proportional deterrence in his 14 January 1963 press conference as follows:

> Moreover, the atomic force has a feature of its own, in that it has an efficacity that is certain and to an extent that is frightening even if it does not approach the conceivable maximum. . . .I only want to say that the French atomic force, from the very beginning of its establishment, will have the sombre and terrible capability of destroying in a few seconds millions and millions of men. This fact cannot fail to have at least some bearing on the intents of any possible aggressor.[3]

This was General de Gaulle's way of telling the world that France would follow the proportional deterrence strategy long advocated by General Pierre Gallois. Proportional deterrence is

_____

[2]Herbert S. Dinerstein, The Politics of NATO Defense Arrangements, p. 5.

[3]Charles de Gaulle, Speeches and Press Conferences, No. 185, p. 11.

simply the term applied to the Gallois argument previously identified as having much to do with the initial decision to produce a French nuclear weapon. The old Gallois thesis that a French capability to destroy as few as 20 Soviet cities would deter Soviet aggression against France was simply restated in a general form. The general statement would be that a lesser power (such as France) can deter a stronger power (such as the USSR) if the lesser power can inflict damage on the stronger power equal to gains the stronger power could make by attacking the lesser power. This strategy is popularly referred to as the "tear off an arm" strategy. The expression comes from the observation that the tearing off of a giant's arm is sufficient to stop his aggression. Both Generals de Gaulle and Gallois have specified that the arm to be torn off is a part of the Soviet population. That is what General de Gaulle referred to when he spoke of the destruction of millions and millions of men. General Gallois says it this way:

> This is why, once directed against the adversary's demographic system, the threat of thermonuclear reprisal assumes its complete significance and acquires a real dissuasive force. The easier it is for the potential victim to materialize this threat, the more the potential aggressor is likely to believe that it will be used. . . .The thermonuclear force can be proportional to the value of the stake it is defending.[4]

In addition, General Gallois has inferred that the required target system is the 48 Russian cities in which 90% of the Russian ruling

---

[4]Pierre Gallois, The Balance of Terror: Strategy For the Nuclear Age, pp. 134 and 137.

30

elite and 50% of the population are concentrated.[5] In summary, the _force de frappe_ is intended to be a retaliatory force targeted against Soviet cities and must be capable of inflicting on the Soviets in a second strike damage equal to that which the Soviets can inflict on France on a first strike.

Another possible strategy for employment of the _force de frappe_, not mentioned officially by French authorities, is that its launch against Soviet targets may serve as an independent "trigger" to the launch of US strategic forces. Since it would be difficult for the Soviets to distinguish between a French attack (albeit small) and the beginnings of an all-out Western strike, the Soviet Union might feel compelled to launch its forces against the West without waiting for clarification. This would be particularly likely if the Soviet force were quite vulnerable. Such diverse experts as General Pierre Gallois and Timothy Stanley, Assistant to the US Secretary of Defense for NATO Force Planning, who agree on little else, agree that the possibility of the French force triggering a US strike is part of the French strategy. Mr. Stanley says:

> Indeed, it is this blackmail potential against the
> United States which the French tacitly rely upon to
> compensate for the unilateral ineffectiveness of their
> national forces in relation to a major power like the
> Soviet Union.[6]

---

[5]Pierre Gallois, "The American Strategic Fallacy," _Atlas_, January 1965, p. 13.

[6]Timothy W. Stanley, _NATO In Transition: The Future of the Atlantic Alliance_, p. 181.

General Gallois cites the example of the British V Bomber force and says:

> Intended to be merely the percussion cap of a terrible exchange of attacks, the dissuasion potential of a nation like Great Britain could indeed be fearful, though limited to only a few weapons. The weapon of the weak, the small atomic arsenal would lead to the use of a large one and to confrontation of the major powers. In France, too, this notion has been advanced to justify French military atomic policy and the concept of security based on a necessarily modest nuclear arsenal.[7]

While the prospects of the "trigger strategy" may be distasteful to the United States, it must be included in US considerations of the force de frappe.

EFFECTIVENESS OF FIRST GENERATION OF THE FORCE DE FRAPPE

The effectiveness of the first generation of the force de frappe is highly dependent on the capability of the Mirage IVA aircraft to reach the Soviet population centers. Since the force will be operated independently by France, it cannot count on being allowed to overfly West Germany on the direct route to the USSR. Likewise, the Mirages must refuel over France or the open sea. These factors probably require that the Mirage combat missions proceed from French bases to refueling areas over the North Sea. Since the force possesses only 12 tankers, more than one refueling per mission is unlikely. Using the ranges of

---

[7]Pierre Gallois, The Balance of Terror: Strategy for the Nuclear Age, p. 139.

Mirage discussed above, the target coverage of the Mirage force relative to the 20 largest population centers in the USSR is summarized on Table I, page 39. This table indicates that on a two way, all high altitude mission from France a Mirage IVA with one refueling over the North Sea can reach only four of the 20 largest population centers in the USSR. This coverage would be reduced if penetration of hostile territory is made at low altitude. Due to this lack of acceptable target coverage, the French will probably be forced to resort to one-way missions with recovery in some country which will hopefully be neutral. Table I shows that 13 of the 20 population centers could be reached on high altitude missions recovering at Helsinki, Finland. Once again this estimate does not allow for use of the optimum tactic, a low altitude penetration of the enemy defenses. The two missions used to compile Table I are shown graphically on Figure I, page 40. Based on this simple analysis, it appears that the effectiveness of the Mirage force with respect to coverage of the targets required by their strategy is poor for two-way high altitude missions and marginal for high altitude missions recovered in Finland.

The next factor in consideration of the effectiveness of the force de frappe is it's vulnerability both on the ground and in flight. Since the force de frappe is required by General de Gaulle's strategy to be a second strike force, it is susceptible to destruction on the ground particularly by Russian ballistic missiles of which there are reportedly some 700 to 800 capable of reaching the French bases.[8] To reduce this vulnerability the French are using four minute strip alert on their main bases and plan to rotate the aircraft randomly between a number of airfields.[9] However, there is little chance of the French receiving warning of a ballistic missile attack. As for defense against attack by air breathing vehicles, the French force is behind the NATO air defense system and can plan on receiving warning and protection from it as long as France remains in NATO. The protection will remain whether France is in NATO or not.

The ability of the Mirage-IVA force to penetrate the Soviet air defenses is highly questionable. Operating independently, the French cannot count on US or NATO measures to suppress the enemy air defenses ahead of their strike aircraft. The range problem previously discussed forces the Mirage to penetrate at high altitude where it is most vulnerable to the modern air defense possessed by the USSR. The only air defense countermeasure mentioned by the French is an electronic countermeasure capability on each aircraft. The marginal range of aircraft also requires that it penetrate directly into the western USSR where air defense is expected to be most concentrated.

While the ability of the Mirage-IVA to reach any substantial number of the Soviet population centers is questionable due to its

---

[8]Institute for Strategic Studies, The Military Balance 1964-1965, p. 3.

[9]Kleiman, op. cit., pp. 100-101.

range and vulnerability, the question of whether one of its 60

kiloton weapons, if it reaches the target, can do the required

degree of damage to such large area targets. While an accurate

calculation of the average probability of damage to the area under

these conditions is impossible on an unclassified basis, it is

fair to assume that more than one weapon must be programmed for

each population center in order to be assured of a reasonable

probability of mission success. The assumption becomes much

more valid when consideration is given to the fact that there is

a finite probability that any programmed weapon will not reach

the bomb release line due to malfunction of the aircraft, attri-

tion by air defense, or gross error by the crew. When the French

planner combines all of the factors with the average probability

of damage to the area target, he will probably find that at least

two weapons must be programmed on each target. Since no accurate

rates are available to make a precise calculation, a theoretical

example must be used to illustrate this point. Suppose that the

French planner finds that the overall probability of mission

success for a single mission is .50. Most likely this is not

high enough to give the commander a reasonable assurance that the

required degree of damage will be done to the target. Then,

additional missions must be applied to this same target. If the

commander requires a probability of mission success of .75 rather than the .50 provided by a single mission, two missions must be assigned.[10]

EFFECTIVENESS OF THE SECOND AND THIRD GENERATIONS

The missiles of the second and third generations of the force de frappe will seek to carry out the same strategy as the aircraft of the first generation. If the ranges of the missiles contained in their original specifications actually materialize, most of the range deficiencies of the Mirage force will be corrected. The surface launched missiles will be able to reach all of the major Soviet population centers west of the Ural Mountains. The submarine launched missiles, if launched from the eastern portion of the Mediterranean, would extend the target coverage a few hundred miles east of the Urals.

The ground and inflight vulnerability problems of the Mirage force will probably be corrected by the missile force unless the Soviets develop effective ballistic missile defense and antisubmarine systems. The major question concerning these missile systems is whether the French are capable of developing and producing such sophisticated ballistic systems. Both programs are still in the development stage and convincing results have not yet been produced.

Even if both missile systems are perfected, the problem of having enough of these systems to form a credible deterrent in the

---

[10]Applying the standard probability equation, $P_S=1-P_F^N$, we find for this example $.75 = 1-.5^N$ or $.5^N = .25$ or $N = 2$. From Probability and Statistics Handout and Problems, Warfare Systems School, pp. 17-18.

minds of the Soviets will remain. Based on the construction plans for missile sites discussed above, the French plan to purchase only 30 operational missiles. If all three of the nuclear power submarines become operational, there will be a total of 48 underwater ballistic missiles by about 1973. Then, it will be 1973 before the French can have as many as 78 ballistic missiles targeted against the Soviet population centers. If the French have only as much difficulty as the United States has had with the reliability and accuracy of first generation missiles, they will certainly have to assign at least two missiles to each target to have a reasonable probability of success. Also, all of the three submarines probably cannot be kept on patrol constantly. It is more likely that only two of the three submarines can be kept on patrol.

In summary, the military capability of the <u>force de frappe</u> seems to suffer from all the deficiencies that the Secretary of Defense ascribed to relatively weak national nuclear forces in his University of Michigan speech of 16 June 1962 when he said:

> In particular, relatively weak national nuclear forces with enemy cities as their targets are not likely to be sufficient to perform even the function of deterrence. If they are small, and perhaps vulnerable on the ground or in the air, or inaccurate, a major antagonist can take a variety of measures to counter them. Indeed, if a major antagonist came to believe there was a substantial likelihood of it being used independently, this force would be inviting a pre-emptive first strike against it. In the event of war, the use of such a

force against the cities of a major nuclear power would
be tantamount to suicide, where its employment against
significant military targets would have a neglibible
effect on the outcome of the conflict.[11]

[11]Robert S. McNamara, "The US and Western Europe," Vital
Speeches of the Day, 1 August 1962, p. 620.

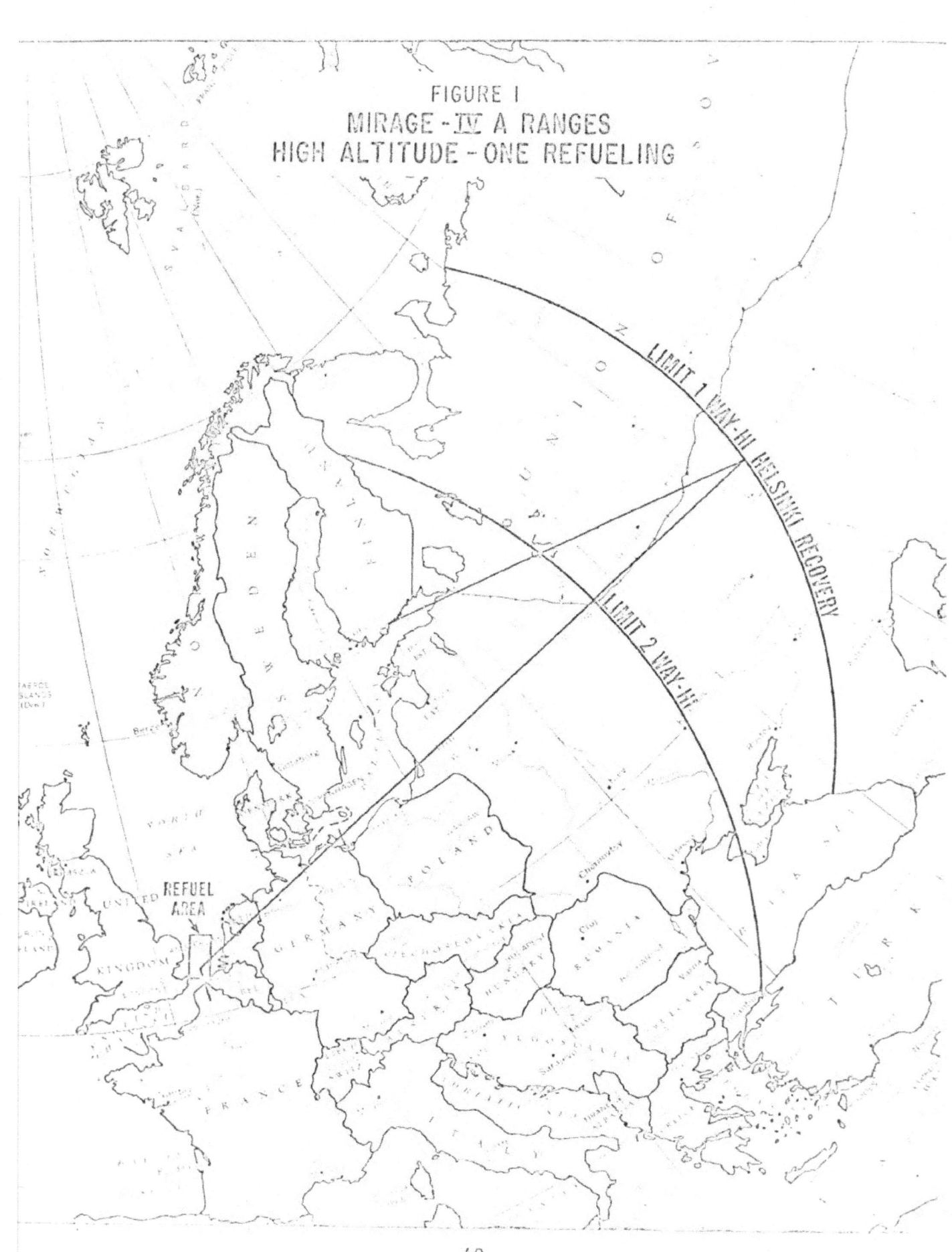

FIGURE I
MIRAGE - IV A RANGES
HIGH ALTITUDE - ONE REFUELING

CHAPTER 5

EFFECTS OF FORCE DE FRAPPE ON US AND NATO STRATEGY

There will apparently be little direct effect on NATO strategy
due to the force de frappe since, according to the French, it will
be employed against Soviet population centers. Since the centers
themselves constitute no threat to the NATO countries, the NATO
commanders are not directly concerned with their targeting. The
existence of the independent Britith deterrent for a number of
years without effect on NATO is an historical example of this
situation. The British Bomber Command was not pledged to NATO
until the Nassau Conference in December 1962.[1] The existence of
a similar force under French control should not effect the NATO
strategy.

What are the effects of the force de frappe on US strategy? From
the effectiveness standpoint of numbers alone, the effect is small.
The French intended to have a force of a maximum of about 100 weapons
targeted on Soviet population centers. The Secretary of Defense told
the NATO Defense Ministers in November 1965 that the US strategic
forces have more than 5,000 weapons, and that the United States has
5,000 more in Europe for NATO use.[2] The Secretary of Defense has also
stated that the United States by the end of June 1965 would have

---

[1]U.S. Dept. of State, "Nassau Comminique of 21 Dec. 1962,"
Dept. of State Bulletin No. 1229, 14 Jan. 1963, p. 44.

[2]Henry Tanner, "5000 A-Warheads Stored for NATO," New York
Times, 28 Nov. 1965, p. 1.

800 Minuteman and 464 Polaris missiles in its operational forces, all of which could be made available for the same mission as the French assign the force de frappe.[3] Under such conditions, it is difficult to identify any effect due to the assignment of about 100 French weapons to the same targets.

The possible effect of the force de frappe that seems to cause most concern to US officials is the possibility that it can be used to trigger a US strategic strike. As discussed above, some experts believe this to be the basic strategy behind the force de frappe. US officials usually refer to this problem indirectly by stating the need for central control of all Western strategic nuclear forces and the fact that the general nuclear war target system is indivisible. Secretary McNamara made these points in his speech at the University of Michigan on 16 June 1962 when he said:

> At the same time, the general strategy I have summarized magnifies the importance of unity of planning, concentration of executive authority, and central direction. There must not be competing and conflicting strategies to meet the contingency of nuclear war. We are convinced that a general nuclear war target system is indivisible, and if, despite all our efforts, nuclear war should occur, our best hope lies in conducting a centrally controlled campaign against all of the enemy's vital nuclear capabilities, while retaining reserve forces, all centrally controlled.[4]

---

[3]Robert S. McNamara, Statement Before the House Armed Services Committee, 18 Feb. 1965, pp. 42-56.

[4]Robert S. McNamara, "The U.S. and Western Europe," Vital Speeches of the Day, 1 Aug. 1962, p. 628.

It seems clear that the central control the Secretary desires means integration of all western strategic nuclear forces in such a way that their independent use is impossible. Professor Henry Kissinger says that the United States preference is that any national forces must be an adjunct to the US strategic forces and, for all practical purposes, subject to American control.[5]

Of course, the _force de frappe_, in no way meets these specifications and was, in fact, created to avoid this control. Then, if the United States is to persist, it must find some way to bring the _force de frappe_ within its central control or modify its strategy to preclude the possibility of being "triggered" by it. To ignore the problem would be to determine that it is inconceivable that the United States could be dragged into a nuclear war against its will by one of her allies such as France. This determination is supported by such experts as Marshal of the RAF Sir John Slessor.[6] However, there is little doubt that, if the French did launch their small force against Soviet population centers, the Soviets would attack US cities in retaliation.

---

[5] Henry A. Kissinger, op. cit., p. 101.
[6] Sir John Slessor, "Nuclear Deterrence In a Changing Strategic Setting," The Royal United Service Institution Journal, Nov. 1964, p. 311.

CHAPTER 6

CONCLUSIONS AND RECOMMENDATIONS

CONCLUSIONS

Since about 1956 France has developed nuclear weapons and the first generation of a military force to deliver those weapons. These accomplishments were made with essentially no assistance from the United States with the only exception being the furnishing of 12 KC-135 tankers late in the program. The nuclear weapon development was virtually all accomplished after France was put on notice by the U S Congress in 1958 that there would be no US "do-it-yourself" kit to put France in the nuclear weapons business.

The pre-de Gaulle motive for initiating the French nuclear weapons program seems to have been simply that no defense was possible without nuclear weapons. With the return to power of General de Gaulle in 1958, the motive changed to the political one that France must have its own nuclear capability to reach de Gaulle's overall objective of making France a major world power and the leader of Western Europe. This goal required that the French nuclear capability be entirely independent and particularly free of any US control. Accordingly, the nuclear weapons are French and their delivery vehicles are French. However, the record does indicate that the French, unofficially at least, requested US assistance in designing and manufacturing nuclear weapons similar to that given to Great Britain. All requests were refused without negotiations due to the general uncooperativeness of the French with the United States. This has resulted in what Timothy Stanley says may be oversimplified and called a vicious circle wherein the United States will not share its nuclear weapons with France because France does not cooperate on an Atlantic basis, and France does not cooperate because the United States does not share its weapons.[1]

The first generation of the _force de frappe_ consisting of Mirage IVA aircraft has now become operational. This force is concluded to be incapable of implementing the French strategy of proportional deterrent against the Soviet Union due to its small numbers, insufficient range, and inability to penetrate defenses. The second and third generations consisting of ballistic missiles may correct many of the present deficiencies but will still not have sufficient numbers to deter the Soviet Union without outside assistance. In addition, these systems are not yet sufficiently developed to justify the judgement that France is capable of perfecting such sophisticated systems without outside assistance. The production of an accurate and reliable ballistic missile, the construction of a nuclear propelled submarine, the mass production of enriched uranium, and the fabrication of an efficient thermonuclear weapon are some of the steps France must take before the second and third generations of the _force de frappe_ become realities.

------

[1]Timothy W. Stanley, _op. cit._, p. 182.

There will be no appreciable direct effect on NATO strategy due to the independent operation of the force de frappe since NATO is not concerned with the population center targets of the force de frappe. The NATO nuclear capability could be significantly improved if the force de frappe could somehow be brought under the operational control of NATO in a manner similar to that existing for the British Bomber Command.

The most significant effect of the force de frappe on overall US strategy is the possibility that the French could use the launch of their force to trigger a launch of a US strike against the Soviet Union. While the likelihood of the French actually doing this may be debatable, the possibility still exists and must be accounted for in the US strategy. It is the conclusion of this writer that this possibility is the main cause of US objections to the force de frappe.

RECOMMENDATIONS

Since the force de frappe is now a fait accompli and the United States can do nothing to prevent it, it is recommended that the United States adopt a policy whereby it will support and assist the development of the force into a militarily effective instrument provided the French place it under some form of NATO control except when vital French national interests are at stake. The first step toward implementing this policy would be to offer France a nuclear weapons assistance agreement under Section 144c of the Atomic Energy Act including the sale of enriched uranium.

The offer would be subject to France's agreeing to a satisfactory NATO control arrangement for the _force de frappe_. In essence, the French would get the same nuclear assistance now given to the United Kingdom and would agree to the same force control arrangements as the United Kingdom has. A separate but equally important agreement would provide the French the necessary US technology to produce reliable and accurate ballistic missiles.

The loudest objection to this recommendation will probably be that the French will reject it because they object to their forces being under NATO control and that the offer is too late. This writer's answer would be that since this offer has never been made to the French, we do not know their reaction. If the underlying cause of French hostility toward the United States is lack of assistance to their nuclear program while the same was given to the British, the offer may be the first step in a new era in United States-French relations. The only thing that the United States has to lose in making such an offer is pride, and the United States has plenty of that.

ARCHIE R. PATTERSON, JR.
Lt Col, USAF

47

BIBLIOGRAPHY

1. Braestrup, Peter. "Atomic Bastille Day in Paris." New York
   Times, 15 Jul. 1965, p. 5.

2. De Gaulle, Charles. President de Gaulle Holds Seventh Press
   Conference. Speeches and Press Conferences No. 185. New
   York: Embassy of France, Press and Information Service,
   14 Jan. 1963. (Vertical File)

3. Embassy of France. Press and Information Service. France and
   its Armed Forces. New York: 1964. (UA700 A35)

4. Embassy of France. Press and Information Service. France's
   First Atomic Explosion. New York: 13 Feb. 1960. (UF767
   F82)

   (A release covering the events leading up to the first
   French atomic test.)

5. Finney, John. "France is Seeking 'Atomic Club' Seat." New
   York Times, 10 Apr. 1960, p. 1.

   (A report of early French efforts to obtain US nuclear
   assistance by Washington's most knowledgeable reporter on
   nuclear matters.)

6. "French Continue Nuclear Delivery Buildup in 6 Year Plan."
   Aviation Week and Space Technology, 15 Mar. 1965, pp. 268-
   271.

7. "French Defense Act Voted." New York Times, 17 Dec. 1964,
   p. 72.

8. "French Deterrent Force Armament Plan." Translations on
   French Nuclear, Missile, Space, and Related Military
   Developments, No. 2, 5 Nov. 1965, p. 26.

   (A JPRS translation of an unsigned article in the French
   language daily newspaper Le Monde, 13 Oct. 1965, p. 8.)

9. Gallois, Pierre M. "The American Strategic Fallacy." Atlas,
   Vol. 9, Jan. 1965, pp. 10-13.

   (Report of an interview with General Gallois.)

10. Gallois, Pierre M. The Balance of Terror: Strategy for the
    Nuclear Age. Boston: Houghton Mifflin, 1961. (U162 G3
    1961)

(The basic source of General Gallois' nuclear strategy.)

11. Glasstone, Samuel, ed. <u>The Effects of Nuclear Weapons</u>.
    Washington: US GPO, 1962.

    (The unclassified effects manual prepared by the U.S.
    Department of Defense and published by the U.S. Atomic
    Energy Commission which lists all announced atomic tests.)

12. "Here is the French Atomic Force." <u>Paris-Match</u>, 11 May 1965,
    pp. I-XVII. (Reprint File)

13. <u>Jane's All World Aircraft, 1965-1966</u>.

    (An excellent source of the characteristics of military
    aircraft.)

14. Kissinger, Henry A. <u>The Troubled Partnership</u>. New York:
    McGraw Hill, 1965. (JX1987 A41 K44)

    (Professor Kissinger's latest appraisal of NATO problems
    including the <u>force de frappe</u>.)

15. Kleinman, Robert. "What France is Out to Get." <u>Reader's
    Digest</u>, Jan. 1964, pp. 100-105.

    (An excellent analysis of the motives behind the <u>force de
    frappe</u>.)

16. Lareymondie, Marc de Lacoste. <u>French Nuclear Power</u>. Washing-
    ton: U.S. Joint Pub. Research Service, 27 May 1964.
    (D844.5 24804)

    (JPRS translation of a series of articles by a former
    employee of the French Atomic Energy Commission which
    appeared in the French language newspaper <u>Le Monde</u> in May
    1964. An excellent and authoritative account of the French
    efforts to develop a nuclear weapon written by one of the
    participants.)

17. Lehmann, Wolfgang J. <u>The Anglo-American "Special" Nuclear
    Relationship Implications and Consequences</u>. Thesis,
    Carlisle Barracks: U.S. Army War College, 3 May 1965.
    (AWC 65-5-100 U)

    (A learned discussion of the US nuclear assistance to the
    United Kingdom including its effects on France.)

18. McNamara, Robert S. <u>The Fiscal Year 1966-70 Defense Program
    and 1966 Defense Budget</u>. Statement before the House Armed
    Services Committee. Washington: U.S. Dept of Defense,
    18 Feb. 1965. (UA23.3 A67 1965a)

19. McNamara, Robert S. "The U.S. and Western Europe." Vital Speeches of the Day, 1 Aug. 1962, pp. 626-629.

    (Text of the Secretary of Defense's address at the University of Michigan on 16 June 1962.)

20. Mendl, Wolf. "The Background of French Nuclear Policy." International Affairs, Jan. 1965, pp. 22-36.

21. "Messmer Explains Objectives of Program." Press Reports and Commentary on French Nuclear Developments and Policy. Washington: U.S. Joint Pub. Research Service, 7 Jan. 1965, pp. 52-56. (D844.5 28192)

    (Translation of an article from LeMonde, 3 Dec. 1964, p. 2.)

22. "New French Nuclear Testing Center in Polynesia." Translations on French Nuclear, Missile, Space, and Related Military Developments, No. 7, 23 Nov. 1965, pp. 1-3. (D844.5 IZ147 no. 7.)

    (A JPRS translation of an article from the French language periodical La Nation, 23 Oct. 1965, p. 4.)

23. Peet, Richard Clayton. "De Gaulle's Force De Dissuasion." Air Force and Space Digest, Jun. 1964, pp. 26-31.

    (A very readable article on the origin, composition and meaning of the force de frappe.)

24. Pergent, J. "Two Thousand French Atomic Bombs in 1970," Press Reports and Commentary on French Nuclear Developments and Policy. Washington: U.S. Joint Pub. Research Service, 7 Jan. 1965, pp. 32-42. (D844.5 28192)

    (Translation of an article from the French language publication Perspectives, 27 Nov. 1964, pp. 1-10.)

25. Rand Corporation. The Politics of NATO Defense Arrangements by Herbert S. Dinerstein, Santa Monica, Feb. 1965. (RAND P-3070)

26. Rand McNally Commercial Atlas and Marketing Guide, 1963.

27. Reboul, Christian. "First Strategic Rocket Bases Will be Ready in 1968." Translations on French Nuclear Missile, Space, and Related Military Developments, No. 1, 2 Nov. 1965, pp. 18-20. (D844.5 IZ147 no. 1)

    (A JPRS translation of an article from the French language newspaper Le Figaro, 15 Oct. 1965, p. 21.)

28. Slessor, John. "Nuclear Deterrence in a Changing Strategic Setting." The Royal United Service Institutional Journal, Nov. 1964, pp. 309-314.

(An excellent appraisal of nuclear weapon control problems by the retired Marshal of the RAF.)

29. Sorenson, Theodore C. Kennedy. New York: Harper and Row, 1965. (E842 S6)

(Contains a clear explanation of President Kennedy's reaction to French nuclear developments and rejection of U.S. nuclear assistance to France.)

30. Stanley, Timothy W. NATO in Transition: The Future of the Atlantic Alliance. New York: Frederick A. Praeger for Council on Foreign Relations, 1965. (JX1987 A41 S73)

(An excellent analysis of NATO problems from the U.S. viewpoint whose author is now Assistant to the Secretary of Defense for NATO Force Planning.)

31. Stanley, Timothy W. "The Gall of Monsieur Gallois." Bulletin of the Atomic Scientists, Oct. 1963, pp. 27-30.

(A U.S. Dept of Defense official answers some of the French criticism of U.S. nuclear strategy.)

32. The Institute for Strategic Studies. The Military Balance 1964-1965. London: 1965. (UA15 I5 1964-1965)

33. U.S. Air Force, Warfare System School. Probability and Statistics Handout and Problems. Maxwell AFB: np.

(A short course in calculating probability of success for aircraft.)

34. U.S. Congress. House. Joint Committee on Atomic Energy. Amendment to the Atomic Energy Act of 1954 as Amended. 85th Congress, 2d Session, House Report 1849. Washington: U.S. GPO, 1958. (HD9698 A3U55 1958a)

35. U.S. Congress. Joint Committee on Atomic Energy. Atomic Energy Legislation Through 88th Congress, 2d Session. Washington: U.S. GPO, 1964. (HD9698 A3U49 1964)

(A precise history of all U.S. atomic energy legislation compiled by the staff of the JCAE.)

36. U.S. Congress. Joint Committee on Atomic Energy. <u>Hearings</u>
     <u>Before the Subcommittee on Agreements for Cooperation of</u>
     <u>JCAE</u>, 85th Congress, 2d Session, Washington: U.S. GPO, 1958.
     (HD9698 A3U55 1958)

37. U.S. Dept of State. <u>Treaties and Other International</u>
     <u>Agreements</u>, Vol. 9, 1958. Washington: 1958. (JS1405 A51
     1958)

38. U.S. Dept of State Bulletin. <u>Nassau Joint Communique with</u>
     <u>Attached Statement on Defense Systems</u>, 21 Dec. 1962. No.
     1229, 14 Jan. 1963, pp. 43-45.

     (The only official report of the Nassau Agreement.)

39. Vichney, Nicholas. "French Science, Technology, and Industry
     Vis-A-Vis the Nuclear Deterrent Force," <u>Press Reports and</u>
     <u>Commentary on French Nuclear Developments and Policy.</u>
     Washington: U.S. Joint Pub. Research Service, 7 Jan. 1965,
     pp. 1-27. (D344.5 28192)

     (A JPRS translation of a series of articles appearing in
     the French language newspaper <u>Le Monde</u> in Nov. and Dec.
     1964.)

40. Zoppo, Ciro E. <u>France as a Nuclear Power</u>. Santa Monica:
     The Rand Corporation, 1962. (RAND P-2485).